How to be a le

By Jenna Wimshurst

© Jenna Wimshurst 2018

Discover other titles by Jenna Wimshurst:

The Suicides

Suicidal Janice

Visit www.jennawimshurst.com for more books, blogs and shenanigans

Thank you for downloading this eBook. This book remains the copyrighted property of the author and may not be redistributed for commercial or non-commercial purposes. If you enjoyed this book, please encourage your friends to download a copy from their favourite authorized retailer. Thank you for your support.

Intro

Welcome to this completely serious (silly) and ridiculously handy (utterly useless) guide on how to be a lesbian. This guide is suitable for: new lesbians - hello and welcome; old lesbians - hello and nice to see you again; and non-lesbians who want to find out how we have sex - hello and either a) stop asking me or b) skip right ahead to Chapter 7 to find out for yourself.

You may think that being a lesbian is simply sleeping with or being sexually attracted to women, but no, there's more to it. It would seem that you have a lot to learn when it comes to being a lesbian, so pay attention, yeah?

Like with many things, lesbianism is thought to have originated in ancient Greek times, however, evidence is
scarce because all surviving sources from the classical period were, without exception, written by men. Of course they were. You'll find throughout this guide that many things regarding gay culture mostly focus on men, but never fear, because I have made my way down into the deep gay hole of the world (interpret that as you will) to find the best bits of lesbian information and have compiled them here for you.

The word lesbian originates from the Greek island of Lesbos where Sappho wrote some downright filthy woman-on-woman poetry. Please note that I don't know whether the poetry was filthy, but I imagine, with all that sun and ouzo, it probably was.

Also, Lesbos, if pronounced incorrectly, is a term many lesbians are often called in the street.

Other slang terms for lesbians include:
Dyke - rumoured to originate from the word hermaphrodite, or the 1940s term bulldyke
Rug or carpet muncher - in honour of the act of cunnilingus, as it were
Doughnut bumper - each to their own; vaginas could look a bit like doughnuts, I guess...
Lezza - a rather unimaginative abbreviation of lesbian
Bean flicker - to flick, rub or massage someone else's clitoris (or your own)
Todger dodger - a woman who dodges the penis
Muff diver - a woman who not-quite-literally dives into muff, also known as a lady garden
Butch - a lesbian who is, quite frankly, butch

Let's have two more interesting facts before we really get started with teaching you how to be a proper lady lover:

- A lavender rhino was the lesbian symbol in the 1970s, and although it was kind of cute, it was also kind of lame, so it hasn't stood the test of time. The idea was that rhinos were docile and misunderstood, but they put up a good fight if they needed to.

- The myth goes that Queen Victoria didn't make female homosexuality illegal when she made male homosexuality illegal. This may or may not have been because she wasn't aware lesbians existed. It might have been because whenever people back in the day heard the term gay they just thought of men bumming instead of women muff diving… and the same often applies today. Or it could be that she actually rather liked the idea of two women together and was actually a big homo herself. Who knows? Not me. Just putting theories out there.

Anyway, on with the guide!

Coming out

It doesn't matter if you come out to your parents when you're 16 or 76 or if they are religious nuts or sceptical atheists, right wingers or left wingers, dead or alive: it's their right as the people who birthed you to know who you are shagging.

Firstly, ensure that your parents are in a place where they are most comfortable, be it the living room, pub or local brothel. If they're at ease then you'll be at ease and it will all go swimmingly, unless it doesn't.

The best thing to do is not to beat around the bush (metaphorical or physical). Just come out with it (eugh, another pun). Perhaps mention other lesbians that your parents know or have seen on the television and compare yourself to them: "You know Clare Balding? Well you know she's a lesbian? So am I". Use a good role model rather than a bad one, so I'd recommend using Balders, rather than someone like Rose West.

Unfortunately, there are some parents that will take the news badly no matter how well you prepare. They'll feel that your desire to not sleep with men is somehow a reflection on their parenting skills. They might blame a particularly tomboyish friend from your past, or your unhealthy interest in things that are "for boys" – things like football, the colour blue or having self-belief in one's own ability, for example.

The only thing to do if this happens is to tell them that you are happy being a lesbian and that your happiness should be worth more than their own comfort levels. If they are still total dicks about the whole thing, then perhaps don't bring up the subject again, emigrate, and become a bit too dependent on alcohol.

You may think that your parents having a good reaction to you coming out as a lesbian would be a great thing, but you'd be wrong. When you go out on a first date with a lady or meet other lesbians you normally swap coming out stories and "they were fine with it" is a bit of a buzz killer. No one wants to hear more about how fine your parents were. Obviously, it's good for you if your parents are fine with it; you'll just have to rely on other interesting parts of your personality to use as an icebreaker.

Once you've come out to your parents that's it for life: you never need to come out again. Well okay, just not for that week anyway. In life you will need to come out a number of times: to colleagues, neighbours, gynaecologists, the lot. It's very simple: you just need to slip the word 'partner' into a sentence, or if you don't have one then follow the tips in the 'butch' section of the next chapter.

Style Guide

When people think of a lesbian they either think of the pretend naked ones in the porn videos, or the fat, short haired, man-looking ones in everyday life. In fact, lesbians come in all shapes and sizes; although some styles are obviously more popular than others. Here are the three main lesbian styles:

Butch: The stereotypical style of choice for lady lovers. Clothing preferences include, but are not limited to: polo shirts, men's short sleeve shirts, men's long sleeve shirts, men's hoodies, men's leather jackets, men's combats, men's baggy jeans, men's boxer shorts and a lovely pair of Dr Martens.

Although style is 80% clothes, it's also 19% attitude and 1% haircut. Haircuts synonymous with butchies are short. Short, short, short. You want long hair? Okay, but only if it's all just one length and there's not even a hint of feathering.

Femme: The opposite to butch is femme, short for femidom. Is it? I don't know, but now that I've put that, it kind of makes sense… Anyway, to be femme is basically to dress, act and appear like a straight girl might, you know, with dresses, make up, ballet pumps etc - just don't sleep with men.

Androgynous: The style that can be hard to get right without looking like the biggest butch out there: the androgynous style. Although it's similar to 'butch', it's a lot subtler and a lot more hipster-ish. Think smart, fitted, black suit, rather than large men's tux. Short hair but with more style and flair.

There's one item of clothing that fits in with all three categories. It's versatile, smart, casual, fitted, baggy and just awesome: the lumberjack shirt. If lesbians were to have a uniform (OMG that would be great and also terrible at the same time) then the lumberjack shirt would definitely be it. However, if any straight girls are reading this then please can you refrain from wearing these shirts as it throws off our gaydar. Thank you kindly.

Interacting with other lesbians

I don't know about other cities in the UK and around the world, but in London the gay district is Soho, and Soho is mainly full of men. So, when you are on the lookout for a nice lady to spend your life (or night) with then you only really have the choice of two bars in London: downstairs at G-A-Y and She Bar, both underground, both very full of sofas.

Unlike in gay male culture, lesbian culture has a more timid approach when it comes to meeting a potential mate. If you're at a bar and you see a nice-looking lady, you don't want to approach her, ask her name, have some banter, then exchange numbers. No. What you want to do is stare at her from across the other side of the room for the entire night. You may then choose to find out her name just for online stalking purposes, but you certainly don't want to appear keen. That's not the lesbian way.

Of course, the most popular way to meet a possible mate is on dating websites/apps. All the dating apps have the gay option, so it's easy to find a wide range of lesbians in your local area. If you're a vegan (statistics say that if you're a lesbian then you're 89.5% more likely to be a vegan) then you're in luck, as there's also a vegan dating app.

The lesbian scene in London can be quite incestuous. I once had two dates lined up with two different women (please note, this doesn't happen often and will probably never happen again) who I met in very different circumstances. One was a fellow stand-up comedian and the other was someone whose friend recommended her on a dating website. Well long, boring story shorter and less boring: they were exes.

It's not uncommon for lesbians to date each other and remain friends after breaking up. It's also not uncommon for friends to be friends for years, then date and then break up and never see each other again because their bad relationship ruined their friendship. Just a word of warning: if you're going to shag your friends then make sure they're not your favourite friend, or you'll be fucked.

Hobbies

Now that you've come out, have chosen a style to follow and have interacted with or stared at another lesbian, it's time to get some hobbies.

Apart from sleeping with women, lesbians have lots of hobbies, most of which can be used as another way of making friends or just knowing if someone is a lesbo or not. For example, you know a girl who goes camping but you're not sure if she's a gay – think of it this way: do you see a bunch of straight women going camping with all their own kit, mallet and all? No, you do not. She's a dyke, my friend. She's a dyke.

Camping: the number one favourite lesbian pastime. If you really want to commit to lady loving then I'm afraid camping is something you'll have to get on board with. Think of it like spending Christmas with the family: no one wants to do it but it's the law, so get on fucking board.

Rules for camping:
- Buy a tent. A big one with at least three compartments: one for sleeping, one for getting changed and one for propping up a little table where you can offer a selection of lesbian tea and biscuits for your fellow lesbian campers.
- Bring warmth. Lots of warmth! Even when you're camping in July it's fucking cold at night, so lots of blankets and a duvet for your blow-up bed is a must.

- Bring food. Lots of it – and preferably stuff that doesn't need to go in the fridge.
- Bring lots of alcohol and games for maximum lesbian fun times.
- Bring other lesbians. Not everything is better with other people but camping is definitely one of them.

If you prefer the warm, comfortable interior of a hotel room rather than sleeping in a field with nothing more than a thin piece of material to protect you, then why not partake in some other hobbies popular with muff divers. These include driving Volvos, walking your dog with other lesbians (dykes with dogs meetup groups are very popular), playing football, doing arts and crafts, origami, carpentry, interior design and rambling.

The lesbians love a good walk and if they can do it with Clare Balding for a BBC Radio 4 special, then what an absolute thrill. What is it about carpet munching that makes women want to go for a long walk along the Jurassic coast line? Beats me.

DIY

There's a very famous saying: give a lesbian a screwdriver and she'll build you a wardrobe. Teach a lesbian to screw and she'll make you a community centre with a large granny annex and horse stables.

It's a fact that gay men teach you contouring, fashion and how to throw shade, and gay women teach you how to install underfloor heating, change a light bulb and utilise your recycling.

Your first toolkit is something rather special but it can be confusing; there are so many tools in B&Q and that's just the staff. Only joking – the staff in B&Q have always been very helpful and friendly when it comes to my purchases. Homebase on the other hand…absolute cunts. Again, this is a joke. Please do not sue me for calling you cunts, instead send me free stuff for promoting your shop. Thank you.

The things you need to buy for your first toolkit:

Screwdriver – make sure it's a magnetic one so that you can put it on your fridge next to your recycling schedule.
Hammer – for putting nails in walls or telling the neighbours to shut the fuck up.
Nails – to give you something to hammer into the wall when you're telling the neighbours to shut the fuck up.

Allen keys – fucking loads of them. You can never have too many in your life.

Pliers – to prize open your girlfriend's cold, cold heart.

Lastly you will need a spanner to tighten up nuts – both metaphorical and physical. You own a tool kit now: you're the boss.

Fantastic. Now that you have your toolkit you need to buy a shit load of paint brushes and at least ten tins of gloss and emulsion paint and paint every wall in your house. Oh, they don't need painting? Don't care. You're a lesbian now and you need to paint your walls, ceilings and skirting boards, and don't forget to varnish every piece of wood furniture you have.

Celebrity knowledge

Our lesbian queen is, of course, Ellen DeGeneres. Those next in line to the throne include Billie-Jean King, Clare Balding and Martina Nav-me-love-some-pavlova.

When I was growing up there were little to no famous lesbians that I knew about. Sure, I'd heard about some woman in America called Ellen, but that was it. But now there are so many more lesbian role models for young girls (and old girls).

From singers to politicians and actresses to sportswomen, here are just some of the most famous and incredible lesbian role models from the UK and America:

Ellen DeGeneres: The most well-known lesbian, everyone knows who she is because she was the first main character to come out as gay in her sitcom in 1997. Plus she has a banging range of suits.

Sandi Toksvig: A brilliant writer, presenter and all round funny woman from the UK.

Clare Balding: Sports presenter and commentator, loves horses and is often seen sniffing around the Olympics.

Sue Perkins: Ex Bake Off TV presenter, one half of Mel & Sue and all round funny writer and performer who has an incredible tomboy style.

Abby Wambach & Megan Rapinoe: Two American football/soccer players and writers who are hot, butch, stylish and just amazing in every way. They also do a lot of social activism.

Jodie Foster: Actress from lots of films including The Silence of The Lambs and Panic Room. Very into yoga and being all zen.

Brandi Carlile: A country (ish) singer and songwriter who is just the most beautiful and incredible woman. I listen to her more than my own wife and if Brandi ever leaves that very ugly/ridiculously beautiful wife of hers then… well…. I'm not sure what will happen but she's my favourite lesbian and let's just leave it at that.

Rosie O'Donnell: Big in the USA, Rosie is an actress, presenter, comedian and general awesome woman. One of the original lesbian comedians.

Portia De Rossi: An Aussie actress who is married to Ellen and who is super femme, proving you can be as feminine and makeup-loving as you want, and still be a lesbian.

Val McDermid: Scottish author of a ridiculous number of best-selling books. The woman is a machine when it comes to writing. I'd also like to go to the pub with her. She seems like a good egg.

Sarah Waters: Another lesbian writer, one that I have been to the pub with. Well, ok it was more that I was in the same lesbian bar that she was in, but still, she's written some of the all-time lesbian classics. E.g. Tipping the velvet.

Samira Wiley & Lea DeLaria: Actresses from Orange is The New Black. One's black, one's white, one's femme, one's butch and they're both brilliant ladies from a fantastic TV show.

Sarah Paulson: Another lesbian actress, Sarah Paulson has been in lots of stuff, my favourite being The People v. O. J. Simpson drama. She seems like she'd also be great craic down the pub.

Hayley Kiyoko: American singer and songwriter, is a big fan of colours and makeup, her fans call her "lesbian Jesus", which although lovely, does sound like quite a lot of pressure…

Jojo Siwa: American Youtuber, Nickelodeon star and general rainbow-on-acid, Jojo Siwa came out in 2021. Some lesbians have short hair and only ever wear dark colours and thankfully Jojo has come along to balance all of that out.

Ruby Rose: An Aussie actress who would look good wearing a dirty bin bag. She was in Batwoman and is sometimes femme, butch, tomboy and gorgeous all at the same time. I hate her…

Lily Tomlin: This comedian and actress is one of my favourites in this list, she's been in 9-5 and Grace and Frankie and she's just the most hippie, jolly and amazingly funny woman.

Katherine Moennig: Another actress, she's from The L Word and she proves that you can be very tomboyish and *still* be a woman/lesbian. I will be inviting her to my pub outing as well.

Lena Waithe: An American filmmaker and actress, I've never seen her before but she's beautiful and I've read that she's a fantastic spokesperson for black and butch lesbians. Wish I looked that good in a suit.

Kate McKinnon: A gorgeous funny lady from SNL and other films like Ghostbusters. She's just one of those annoyingly talented, good looking women who I would say is the "Ellen" of today. Kind of.

Hannah Gadsby: A comedian from DAN UNDA, who was made even more successful after her Netflix special, Nanette. She's a lesbian but only identifies as tired. She also isn't a fan of the LGBT flag but is a fan of a good suit.

Wanda Sykes & Jane Lynch: Two comedians and actresses from the USA, both very funny and have both featured in my favourite TV show of all time… Will & Grace.

Billie Jean King: An ex-professional tennis player, generally amazing woman and social activist. She won "**The Battle of the Sexes**" and broke endless tennis records.

Martina Navratilova: Another incredible tennis player who fights for women and lesbian rights and has won a stupid amount of tournaments. She's one of the lesbian community's best people.

Cynthia Nixon: Actress from Sex and The City. Super femme and beautiful plus she ran for governor of New York. (These lesbos are just amazing, yes they're singers, actresses and models but they are also activist and politicians pushing for change and progress. Oh stop it, I'm going to cry!)

Ruth Davidson, Kezia Dugdale, Joanna Cherry & Angela Eagle: Just a few of the incredible lesbian politicians from all areas of the British political spectrum. You may not agree with all of their politics but these women are such amazing role models for young people showing that gay women can be the leader of a political party. Well you can in Scotland, the rest of the UK needs to bloody well catch up.

Nicola Adams: This incredible boxer was the first celebrity to dance in a same sex couple on Strictly Come Dancing and not only is she an incredible athlete but she's the sweetest person on the telly.

Fiona Shaw: Actress who played Aunt Petunia and that hilarious woman from Killing Eve, Fiona Shaw seems like the most amazing woman to talk to and her wife, Sonali Deraniyagala, is a writer who has the most heart-breaking and incredible story.

Miriam Margolyes: A most insane, crazy and ridiculously wonderful actress who doesn't take any crap from anyone, she is very much an honest person who is funny and very inspiring when it comes to not taking life or people too seriously.

KD Lang: A true iconic lesbian singer from a few years ago. My friend watched an entire interview with her on The Graham Norton Show and she didn't believe that she wasn't a man.

Melissa Etheridge: An American country singer, songwriter and activist, I've only just started to listen and learn about her but what I can tell so far is that she makes cracking music, is a good egg and can also come to the pub with the other lesbos I've mentioned.

Gina Yashere: Gina is a funny lady from the UK who has been on the UK comedy circuit for quite a few years. She's recently branched out in the US where she's just doing ridiculous well and has 3 Netflix specials.

Liz Carr: This comedian, actress and disability activist is most famous in the UK for staring in Silent Witness where her sarcastic facial expressions and reactions are something we can all aspire to.

DISCLAIMER: This list of women are who I believe have publicly identified themselves as lesbians. This list was updated in March 2021 and was believed to be correct at the time of publishing.

The Lesbian Bible

If you haven't already binged watched 'The L Word'? Then what the fuck are you doing?! Oh, you're reading this very useful lesbian guide. I'll let you off then. Once you've finished this spiffing piece of informative writing, I suggest you rush to your local Blockbuster and rent all six seasons immediately.

Why? Well because many of us lesbos learnt our morals and ethics from watching the show. 'Tis our Bible, our Quran, our Torah, our blueprint. Some things that you will learn about lesbians from watching 'The L Word' include: lesbians are terrible lesbians at the start. You think that the hot, lesbian serial dater in your town was born a goddess of all things muff diving? No, when she first came out she was the same frigid, cold, bloated, ugly lesbian that you probably are.

All lesbians are rich. Filthy rich. It's a fact and it's represented really well on 'The L Word'. Everyone has huge fuck off houses, designer clobber and spends most of their time in a cafe. Clearly no one has a job and those that do work only a three-hour month. The dream.

Sex

Finally, the sexy chapter. Depending on where you live and how old you are, people may or may not ask you how lesbians have sex. Simply tell them that it involves a chicken, two metres of blue string and a half-eaten bag of jelly babies and leave it at that.

So, how do we have sex? Well you can choose to penetrate another lady with your fingers, fists, arms or entire body – depending on the size of you and the size of her vagina. You might like to buy a dildo or a strapon from a sex shop or online shop that promises total discretion. You can also buy them on Amazon Prime but there's nothing particularly discrete about Priming a whopping 10" cock for next-day delivery.

Scissoring is not a thing. Not for me anyway. Other people may do it but it looks awkward as fuck, and you end up looking like you're pretending to have a fit while getting kicked in the face.

The main important thing you need to remember when thinking or doing lesbian sex is that there are no guys in it, and I don't mean that there are no actual guys (because obviously there aren't). I mean that when some dickhead asks which one is "the man" it means they are too heavily invested in gender roles, and lesbian sex doesn't have gender roles. Sausage rolls, people, not gender roles.

Like with heterosexual sex, everything in lesbian sex is and can be covered just the same; the only difference is that there's no sperm and no risk of getting pregnant. Yay! What a turn on.

Whether it's anal, oral, penetrative or some proper weird shit, as a lesbian you can have sex however the fuck you want. Just don't do it with a man because that means that you're bisexual and this is a book for lesbians. Only joking – this is a book for everyone! Don't get your bisexual rainbow braces in a twist.

One big misconception about lesbians is that we know what the other likes immediately just because we've got the same bits. This is fake news, people. Fake. News. Sad! Like with straight couples, it can take a while for the sex to be good and to find what each other likes and doesn't like.

Unlike with straight couples, both parties normally orgasm and then end on a cuddle where at least one of them cries because they love each other so much. I once read a joke that said "if babies were made only when the woman had an orgasm then there'd be less than six people in the world". What a stereotypical, lazy and utterly hilarious thing to say.

Lesbian sex terminology:
Gold star – you've never had sex with a man,
Lesbian bed death – you and your partner stop or rarely have sex,
Pillow princess – a lesbian who likes to lay there and get all the good stuff but doesn't actually reciprocate it,
Funch – a quick shag at lunch, wonderful.

Tearing the homophobes a new one

Now that you're a proper lezzy lesbo you not only get to enjoy all the lesbian things in life but you also get to enjoy all the anti-lesbian things in life e.g. Bible bashing homophobes.

Please note that not all homophobes bash Bibles. Some bash the Torah, the Quran or any other religious text of their choosing.

You're not going to win every argument you have with a homophobe, but you will win most of them by using hard facts and wit:

Example 1
Homophobe: "The Bible says being gay is wrong"
You: "The Bible also says that it's a sin to wear mixed fabrics and eat shellfish so I suggest you take all your clothes off, you fishy prick."

Example 2
Homophobe: "What you do in the bedroom is disgusting."
You: "Do you not go down on your wife? / Does your husband not go down on you? You poor thing! You really must try it; it feels nice and it won't end up in unwanted pregnancies that drain the state and add to our already overpopulated planet."

Example 3

Homophobe: "Being a lesbian is a choice."

You: "Being a cunt is a choice and you seem to have chosen very poorly indeed. Now excuse me while I go bump doughnuts with my girlfriend."

Example 4

Homophobe: "You're a lesbian because no men will have you."

You: "No, I'm a lesbian because although I don't hate men, I don't want their genitalia anywhere near me. But thanks for your concern."

Congratulations! You have now reached the end of this very useless lesbian guide and are ready to go out into the world as a proper lady lover. Thank you very much for reading this satirical guide on how to be a lesbian, I hope you got at least one small piece of useful information. Either way, you are now ready to go and lez your way through life, dear child!

Discover other titles by Jenna Wimshurst:

The Suicides

Suicidal Janice

Visit www.jennawimshurst.com for more books, blogs and shenanigans

Printed in Great Britain
by Amazon